MY COLOR CHART

red

green

yellow

purple

blue

brown

pink

orange

gray

white

black

me   and   my friend

My eyes are

My hair is

His (Her) eyes are

His (Her) hair is

I'm finished!

I win!

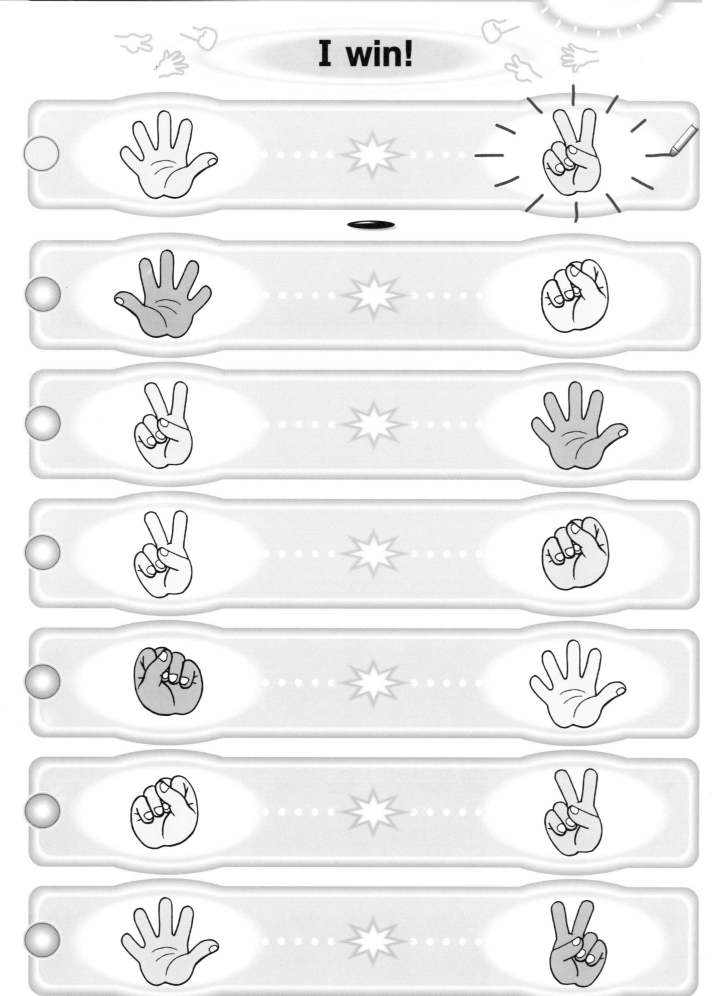

How many ~ ?

1

2

3

4

5

6

one

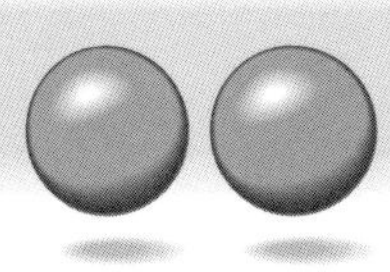

two

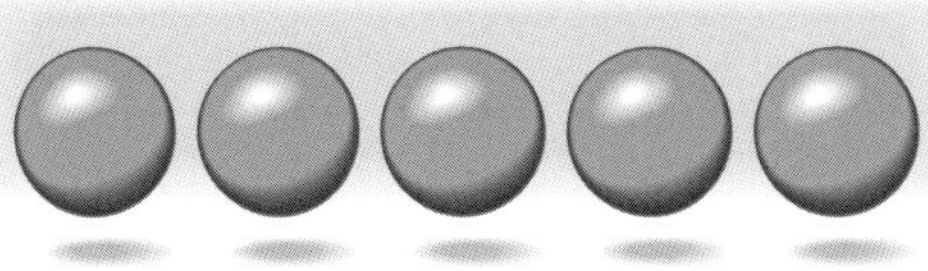

three

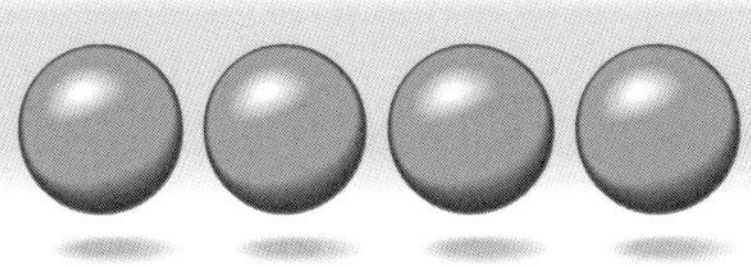

four

five

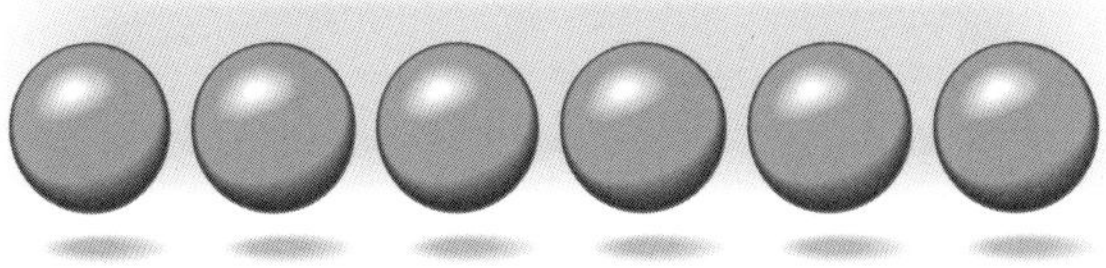

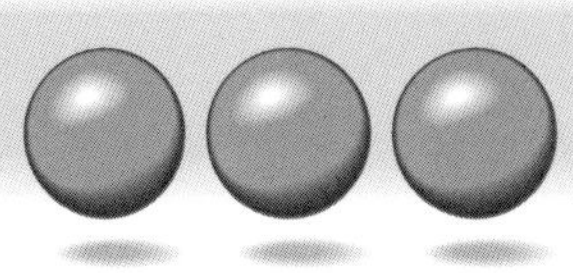

six

Color five.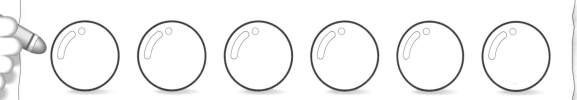

Color two.

Color three.

Color six.

Color one.

Color four.

I'm finished!

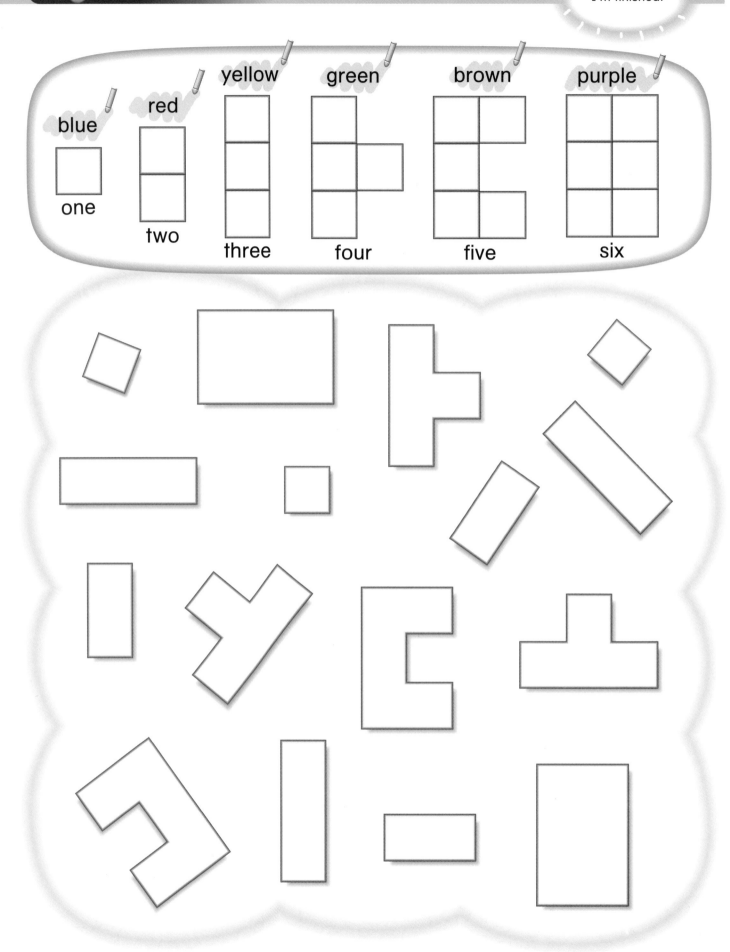

blue
one

red
two

yellow
three

green
four

brown
five

purple
six

同じ形のブロックを見つけて色をぬろう。
Find the shapes and color them.

I'm finished!

Color the castle.

▭ ┈➤ ✏️ orange	◯ ┈➤ ✏️ yellow
◻ ┈➤ ✏️ blue	△ ┈➤ ✏️ red

How many ▭ ?

How many ◻ ?

How many ◯ ?

How many △ ?

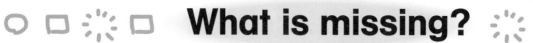

What is missing?

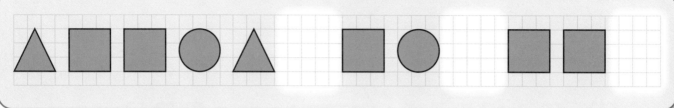

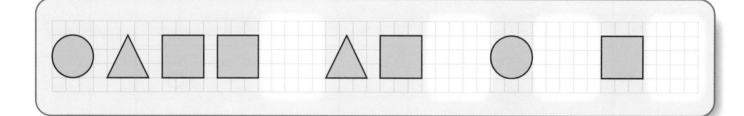

Find the same pattern.

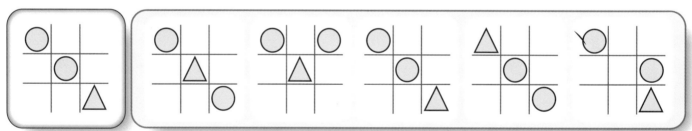

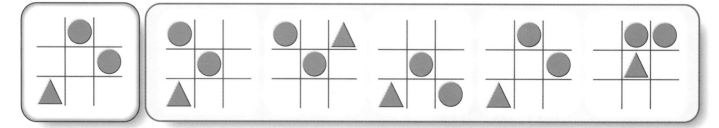

Maze

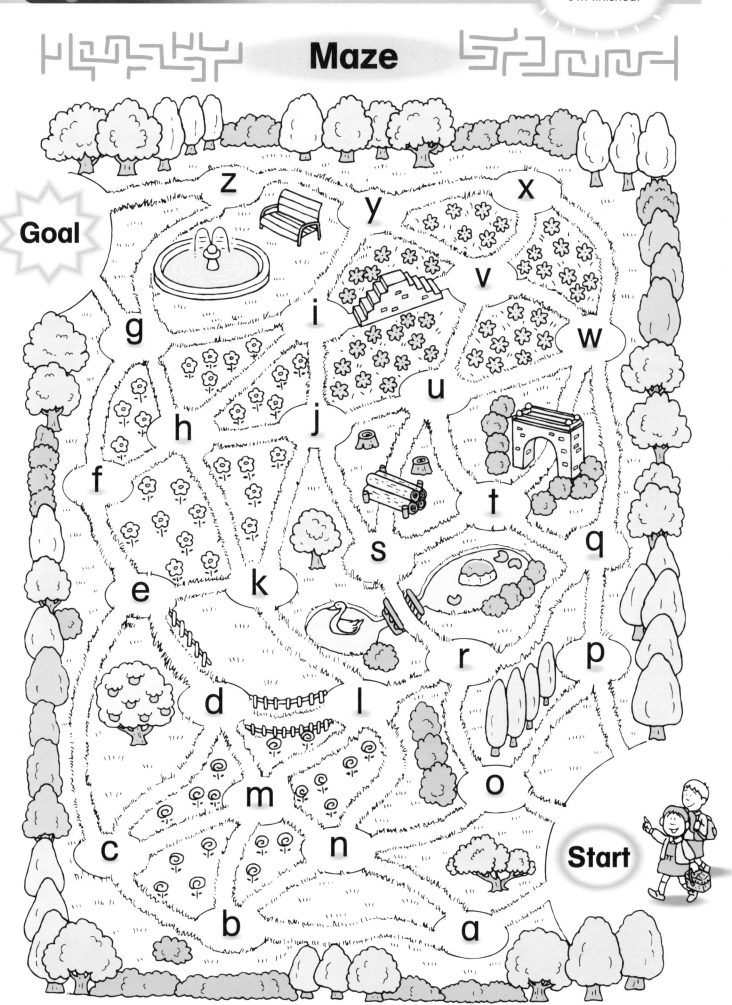

Goal

Start

Color the animals.

a little yellow dog

a big green dog

a little black cat

a big orange cat

a little purple rabbit

a big pink rabbit

a little brown dinosaur

a big gray dinosaur

dog   cat   rabbit   dinosaur

10

I'm finished!

What is it?

dog

rabbit

dinosaur

cat

boy

girl

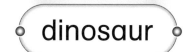
dinosaur

dog

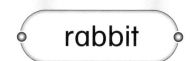
rabbit

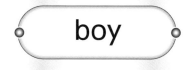
boy

girl

cat

I'm finished!

Let's make a zoo!

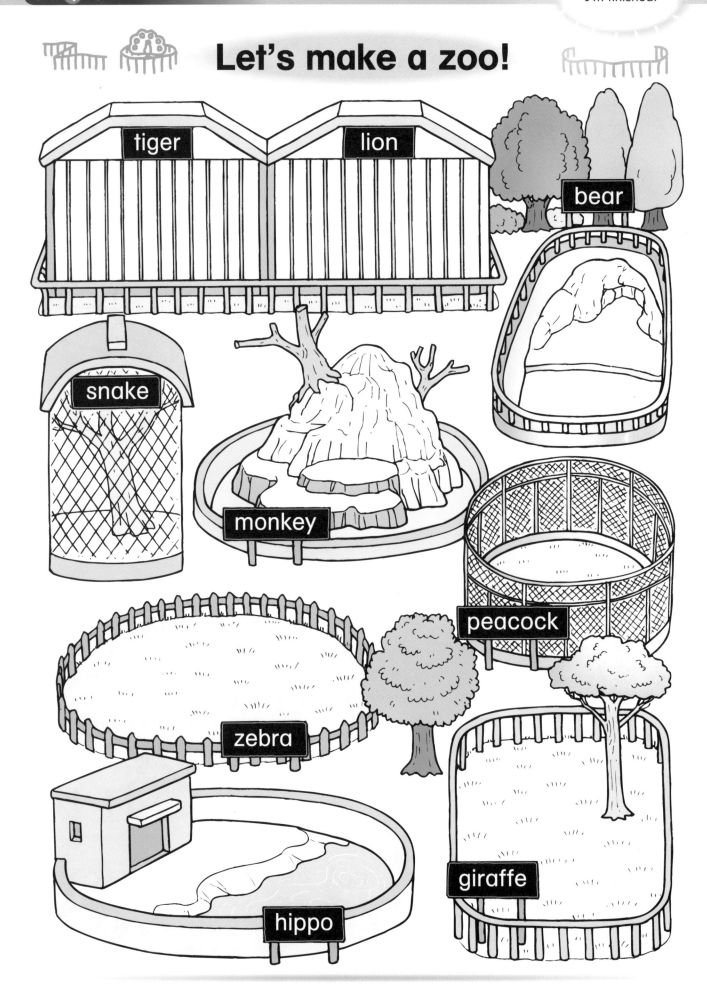

Cut out the animals on p.31. Color them and glue them in the appropriate places.

I'm finished!

My family member

Draw one member of your family in the frame.

I'm finished!

Whose is this?

Look at pp.18-19 of the text for a while. Then close the text and match the items with the characters.

on   in

on   in

on   in

on   in

on   in

on   in

I'm finished!

   # This is my dinner!

I am full.

Cut out food and drinks on p.29. Children color and glue the food they want on the table.
Have children explain what they have on the table.

I'm finished!

a green onion

a pink tomato

a red carrot

a yellow cucumber

a brown potato

one

two

three

four

five

 one two three  four  five

A funny salad!

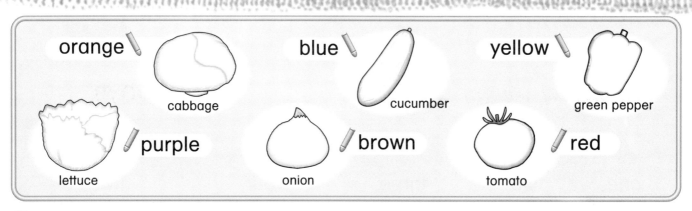

orange cabbage

blue cucumber

yellow green pepper

purple lettuce

brown onion

red tomato

I'm finished!

 # Find and color.

 → blue    → green   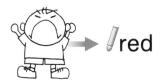 → red

How many ? [ ] sad boys.

How many ? [ ] angry boys.

How many ? [ ] happy boys.

I'm finished!

I am _____ when

I am _____ when

I am _____ when

I am _____ when

I am _____ when

Think and draw by yourself.

| happy | angry | sad | scared |

20

I'm finished!

Color the monster.

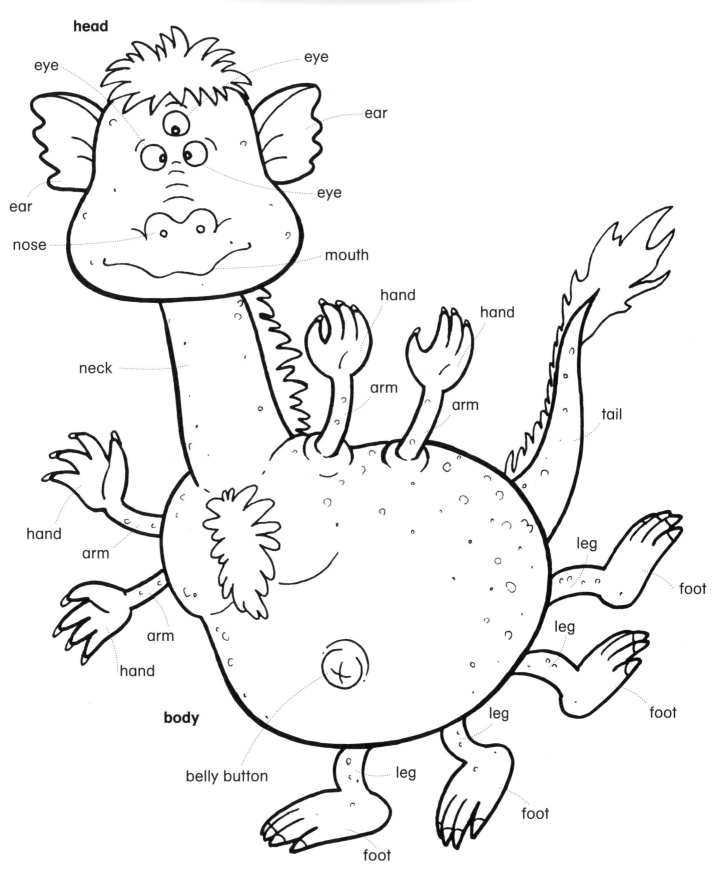

head

eye   eye

ear

ear

eye

nose   mouth

hand   hand

neck   arm   arm   tail

hand   leg   foot

arm   leg

arm   leg   foot

hand

body   leg   foot

belly button   leg

foot

foot

Color each part of the body.
Ask questions: ●How many eyes? ●What color is the nose? ....

I'm finished!

What is missing?

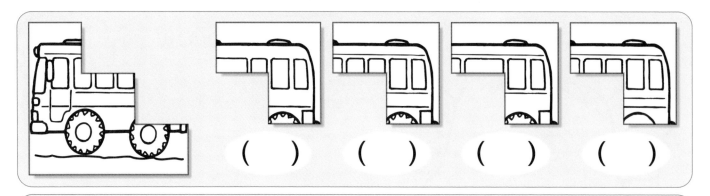

(　　)　　(　　)　　(　　)　　(　　)

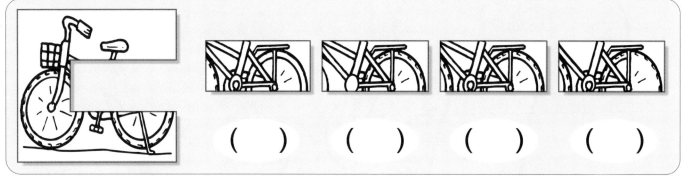

(　　)　　(　　)　　(　　)　　(　　)

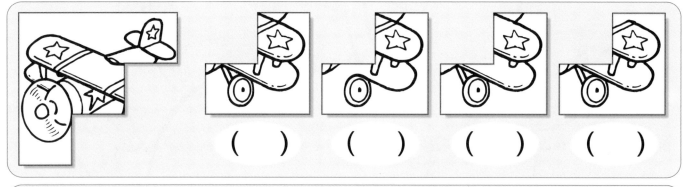

(　　)　　(　　)　　(　　)　　(　　)

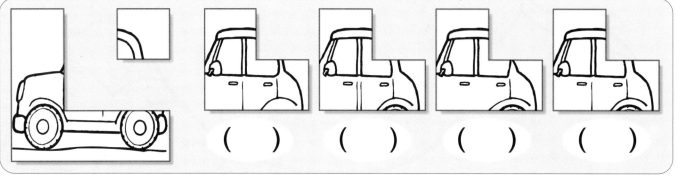

(　　)　　(　　)　　(　　)　　(　　)

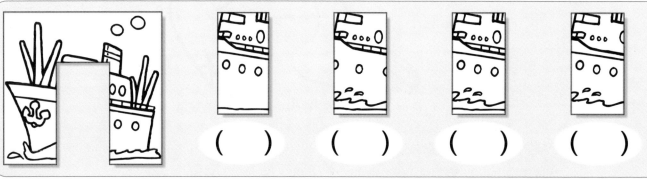

(　　)　　(　　)　　(　　)　　(　　)

I'm finished!

Where are the animals?

blue

brown

yellow

pink

green

purple

on    in   under

Where were the animals?

まえのページの絵をおぼえているかな？

Color the animals the same as they are on p.23 and connect them to the correct place.
Ask questions: ●Where is the dog? ●What color is the dog? ....

I'm finished!

  # Say and color.

Practice saying the words and color the pictures.

Find and color.

spring	→ pink	summer	→ yellow
fall	→ orange	winter	→ green

Action Bingo

See p.28.

How to use the Supplements

Action Bingo (p.27)

1 Cut out the pictures on p.27 and have children make their own Bingo board. The ⭐ can be used in any square.

2 Let's play Action Bingo!!

Supplement ❶   ## This is my dinner! (p.16)

1 Cut out the food on p.29.

2 Children color and glue the food they want on the table.

3 Have children explain what they have on the table.

Supplement ❷   ## Let's make a zoo! (p.12)

1 Children cut out the animals on p.31.

2 Color the animals and glue them in the appropriate places in the zoo.

Supplement 1

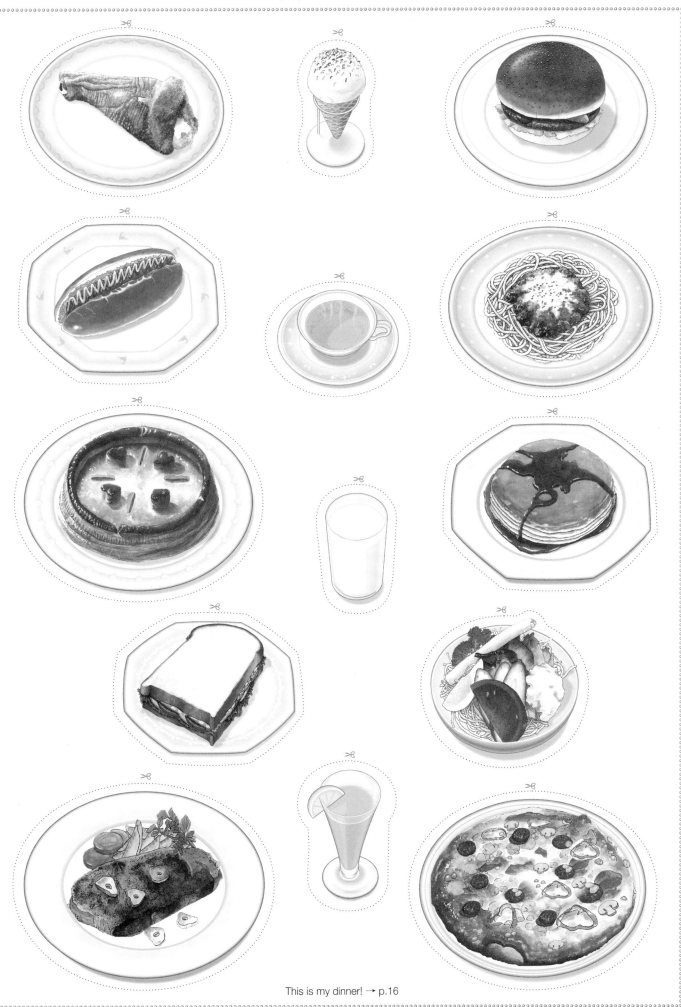

This is my dinner! → p.16

Supplement ②

Let's make a zoo. → p.12